RECORDED VERSIONS
GUITAR
AUTHENTIC TRANSCRIPTIONS
WITH NOTES AND TABLATURE

PATTY GRIFFIN
children running through

Music transcriptions by Pete Billmann

ISBN 978-1-4234-5373-4

HAL•LEONARD®
CORPORATION

7777 W. BLUEMOUND RD. P.O. BOX 13819 MILWAUKEE, WI 53213

In Australia Contact:
Hal Leonard Australia Pty. Ltd.
4 Lentara Court
Cheltenham, Victoria, 3192 Australia
Email: ausadmin@halleonard.com.au

Visit Hal Leonard Online at
www.halleonard.com

You'll Remember

Words and Music by Patty Griffin

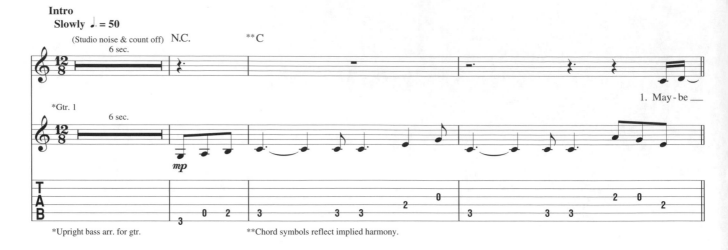

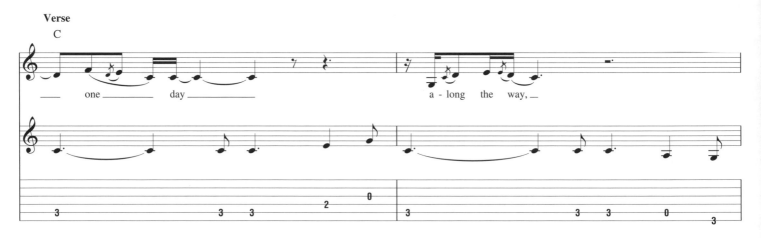

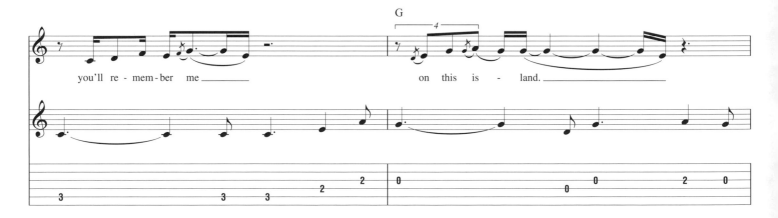

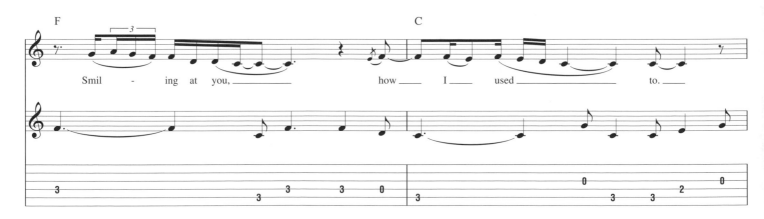

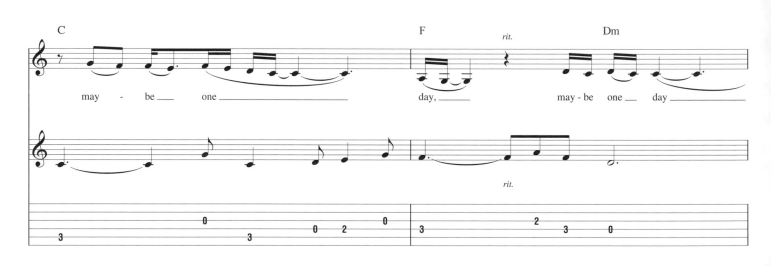

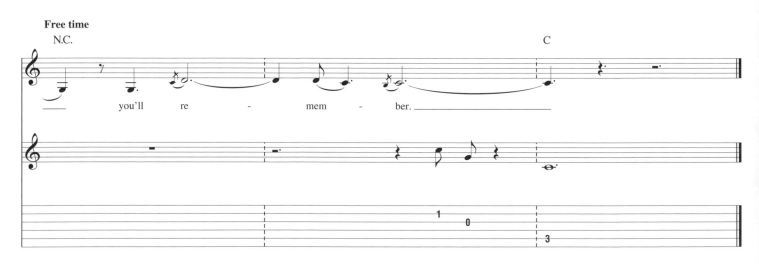

Stay on the Ride

Words and Music by Patty Griffin

"That's o-kay, I'll stand.

I might look like a lit-tle old __ man to you, __ but I've been rid-ing this bus __ for years __ and years and __ years. __

I don't e-ven know where it's go-ing to." And the driv-er said, "You don't know where this bus is go-ing to?"

Old man says, __ "No I don't, __ do you?" __ Driv-er says, "You don't know where this bus __ is go-ing to?"

G#7
(E7)

Old man says, "I just want it to get me __ through." __ Hey, hey, I'm a,

Gtr. 1

Rhy. Fig. 3   End Rhy. Fig. 3

%‌ Chorus

C#7   D#7   G#7
(A7)   (B7)   (E7)

{1., 2. stay-ing} on the ride. __   It's gon-na take {1., 2. me} some-where. __   {1.
 3. stay   }   {3. you }   {2. Hey, hey, __ hey.
                                                                                       3. Hey, hey, __ hey.

Rhy. Fig. 4   End Rhy. Fig. 4

And the old man said, "No I don't, son, _____

D.S. al Coda 1

Gtr. 1: w/ Rhy. Fig. 3

G#7
(E7)

but I'm hap - py to go." _____ Hey, hey, hey, _____ I'm

⊕ **Coda 1**

Gtr. 1: w/ Rhy. Fig. 2 (1st 2 meas.)

G#m7
(Em7)

- where, _____ some - where, _____ some - where, _____ some - where, _____

G#7
(E7)

some - where. _____ I was born _____

Gtr. 1

Bridge

Gtr. 1: w/ Rhy. Fig. 4

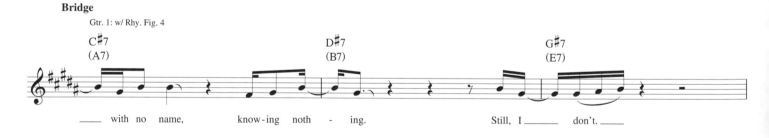

C#7   D#7   G#7
(A7)   (B7)   (E7)

_____ with no name,   know - ing noth - ing.   Still, I _____ don't. _____

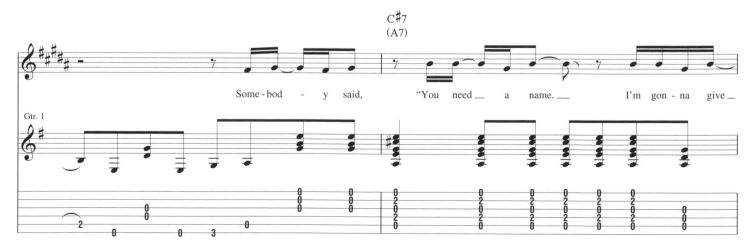

C#7
(A7)

Some - bod - y said,   "You need _____ a name. _____ I'm gon - na give _____

Gtr. 1

Gtr. 1: w/ Rhy. Fig. 3

G#7
(E7)

May - be it is." And he said, uh,

⊕ Coda 2

Outro

Gtr. 1: w/ Rhy. Fig. 2 (1 1/4 times)

G#m7
(Em7)

—— where. __ It al - ways takes you some - where, bound to take you some -

- where, __ al - ways takes you some - where, got - ta take you some -

- where, al - ways takes you some - where, bound to take you some -

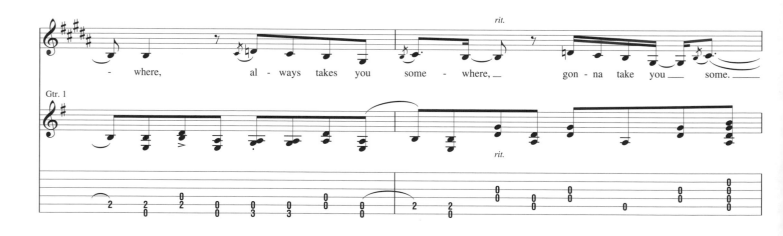

rit.

- where, al - ways takes you some - where, __ gon - na take you __ some. __

Gtr. 1

rit.

G#7
(E7)

Trapeze

Words and Music by Patty Griffin

Capo III

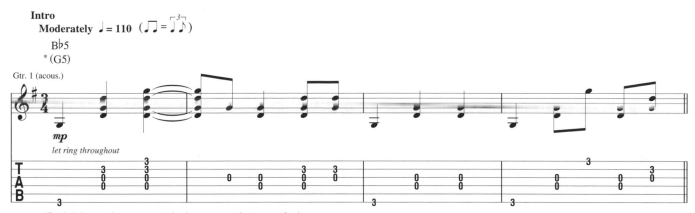

*Symbols in parentheses represent chord names respective to capoed guitar.
Symbols above reflect actual sounding chords. Capoed fret is "0" in tab.
Chord symbols reflect implied harmony.

gave her a po - tion and she ___ drank it in. ___

Gtr. 1: w/ Rhy. Fig. 2

Af - ter that, ___ her

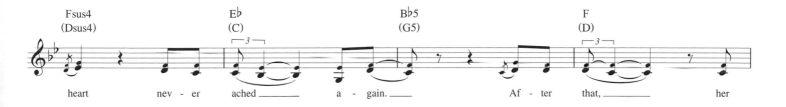

heart nev - er ached ___ a - gain. ___ Af - ter that, ___ her

Gtr. 1: w/ Rhy. Fig. 4

heart nev - er ached ___ a - gain. ___ Some

Chorus

peo - ple don't ___ care ___ if they live ___ or they die. ___ Some

Gtr. 1: w/ Rhy. Fig. 5

peo - ple wan - na know ___ what it ___ feels ___ like to fly. ___

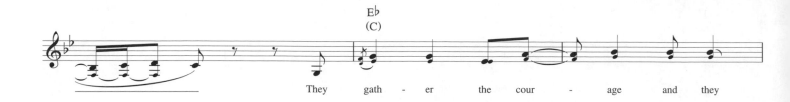

They gath - er the cour - age and they

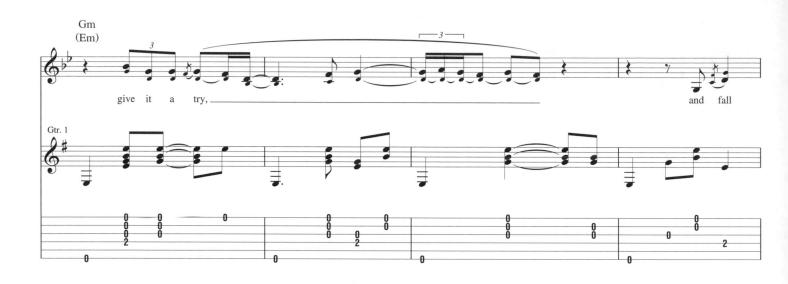

give it a try, and fall

Gtr. 1

un - der the wheels of the time go - ing by.

D.S. al Coda

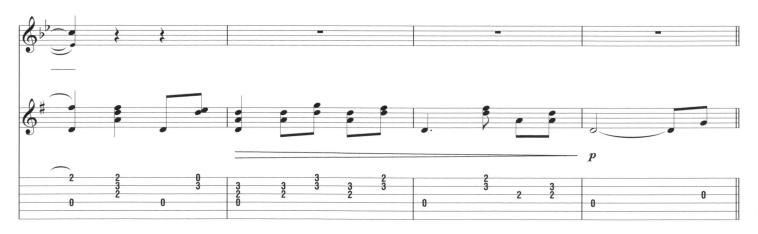

p

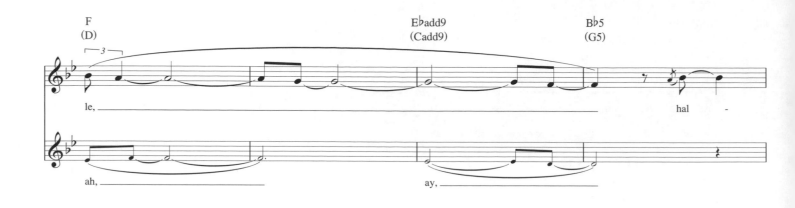

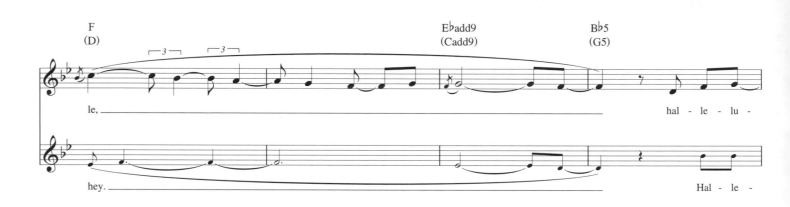

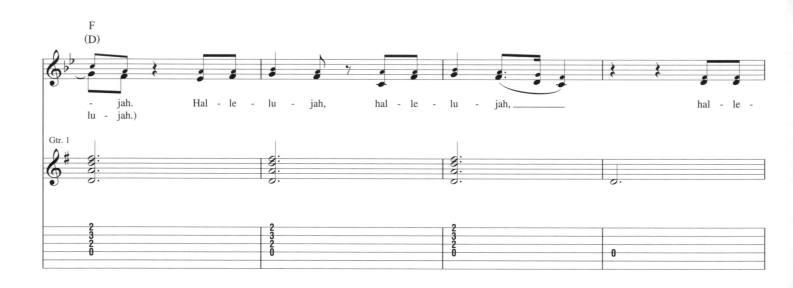

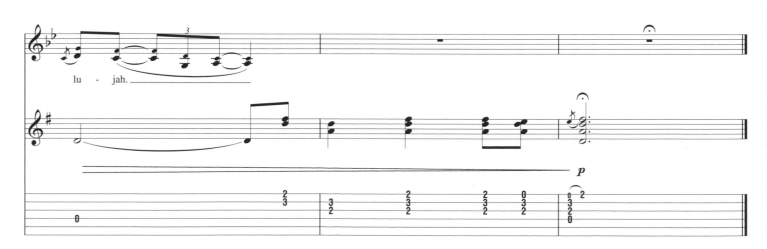

Getting Ready

Words and Music by Patty Griffin

Gtr. 1: Open D5 tuning, Capo III:
(low to high) D-A-D-D-A-D

Gtr. 2: Capo I

(D5)   (F6)   (Gsus2)

Intro
Fast Rock ♩ = 210

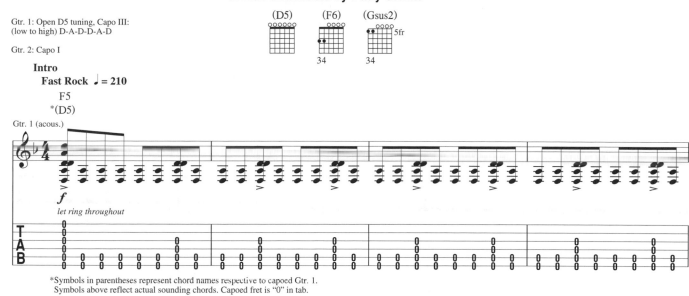

Gtr. 1 (acous.)

f   *let ring throughout*

*Symbols in parentheses represent chord names respective to capoed Gtr. 1.
Symbols above reflect actual sounding chords. Capoed fret is "0" in tab.

Rhy. Fig. 1   A♭6(no3rd) F5   (F6(no3rd)) (D5)   **End Rhy. Fig. 1**

Verse
Gtr. 1: w/ Rhy. Fig. 1 (4 times)

F5   A♭6(no3rd) F5
(D5)   (F6(no3rd)) (D5)

1. Oh, ba - by, I'm get - ting read - y.

A♭6(no3rd) F5
(F6(no3rd)) (D5)

I'm get - ting read - y to let _____ you go. _____ My

A♭6(no3rd) F5
(F6(no3rd)) (D5)

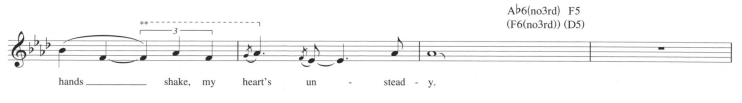

hands _____ shake, my heart's un - stead - y.

**Sung behind the beat.

*Symbols in double parentheses represenet chord names respective to capoed Gtr. 2.
Symbols above represent actual sounding chords. Capoed fret is "0" in tab.

Guitar Solo

Gtr. 1: w/ Rhy. Fig. 3 (2 times)

F5	A♭6	B♭sus2	A♭6	F5	A♭6	B♭sus2	A♭6
(D5)	(F6)	(Gsus2)	(F6)	(D5)	(F6)	(Gsus2)	(F6)

Gtr. 2 ((E5))   ((G6))   ((Asus2))   ((G6))   ((E5))   ((G6))   ((Asus2))   ((G6))

w/ dist.
1/2

F5	A♭6	B♭sus2	A♭6	F5	A♭6	B♭sus2	A♭6
(D5)	(F6)	(Gsus2)	(F6)	(D5)	(F6)	(Gsus2)	(F6)
((E5))	((G6))	((Asus2))	((G6))	((E5))	((G6))	((Asus2))	((G6))

1/2   P.H.   *fdbk.   1/4
                           w/ bar

Pitch: G♯   E

*Microphonic fdbk., not caused by string vibration.

Verse

Gtr. 1: w/ Rhy. Fig. 3 (6 times)

F5	A♭6	B♭sus2	A♭6	F5	A♭6	B♭sus2	A♭6
(D5)	(F6)	(Gsus2)	(F6)	(D5)	(F6)	(Gsus2)	(F6)
((E5))	((G6))	((Asus2))	((G6))	((E5))	((G6))	((Asus2))	((G6))

3. Ba - by, ba - by,   got   no   trac - tion. _____   I   was

⊕ Coda

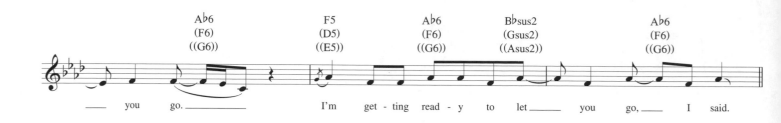

I'm get - ting read - y to let____ you go.____ I'm get - ting read - y to let____

____ you go.____ I'm get - ting read - y to let____ you go,____ I said.

Outro

Gtrs. 1 & 2: w/ Rhy. Figs. 5 & 5A

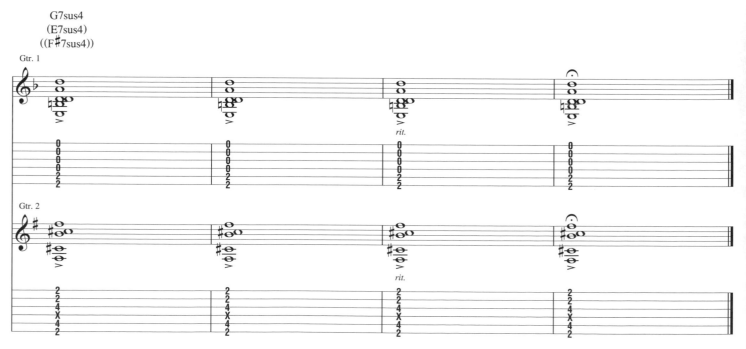

Burgundy Shoes

Words and Music by Patty Griffin

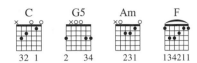

In your red lip-stick and ___ li-lac ker-chief, you're the most ___ pret-ty ___ la - dy in the world.

End Riff A

Sun. ___

2. The

Verse

Gtr. 1: w/ Riff A

bus driv-er smiles, ___ a dime ___ and a nick - el. We climb on our ___ seats, the vi - nyl is cold.

"Mi-chelle Ma Belle," a song ___ that you ___ loved ___ then. ___ You hold my hand and sing to your-self.

Chorus

Rhy. Fig. 1

Gtr. 2
(acous.)

mf

let ring throughout

Sun, ___ sun, ___

Gtr. 1

mf

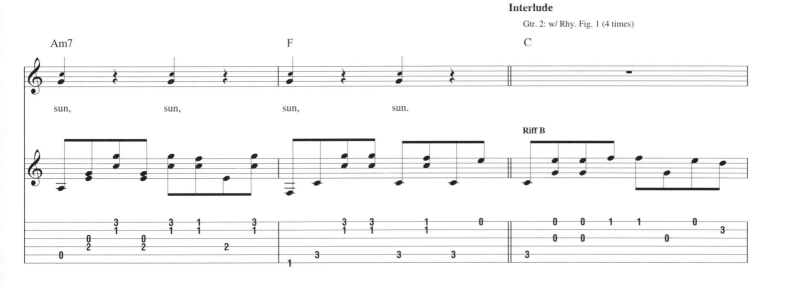

Interlude

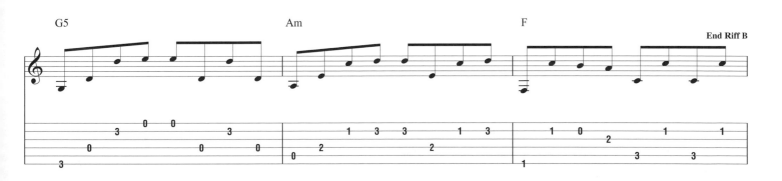

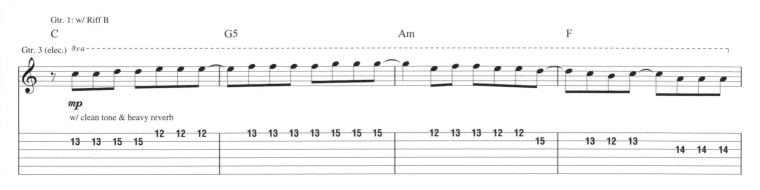

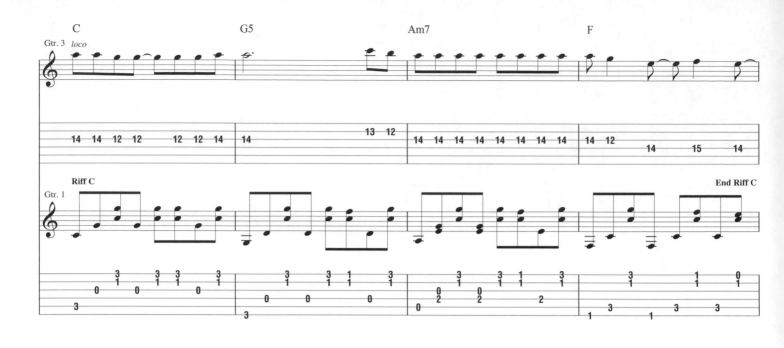

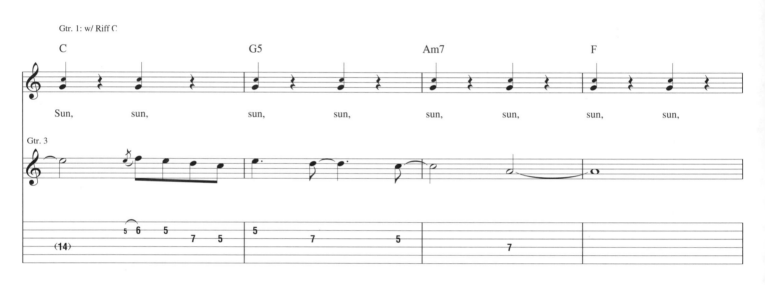

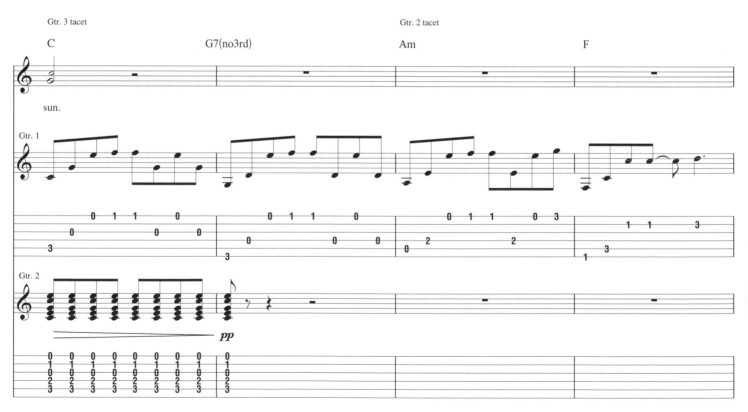

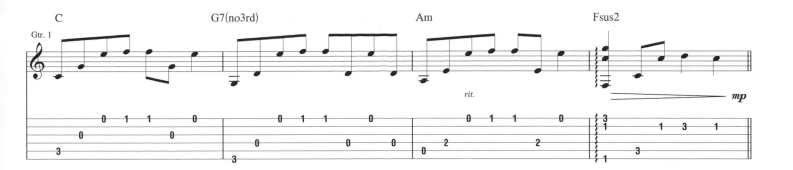

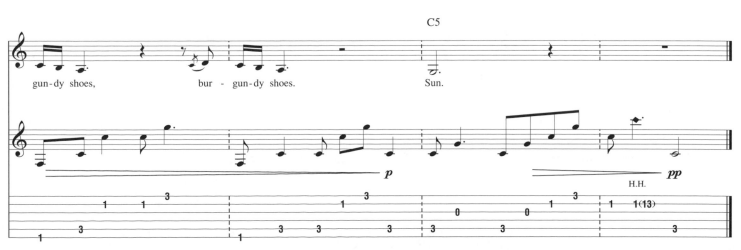

Heavenly Day

Words and Music by Patty Griffin

Capo IV

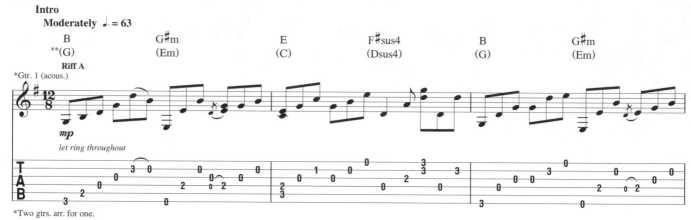

*Two gtrs. arr. for one.

**Symbols in parentheses represent chord names respective to capoed guitar.
Symbols above reflect actual sounding chords. Capoed fret is "0" in tab.
Chord symbols reflect implied harmony.

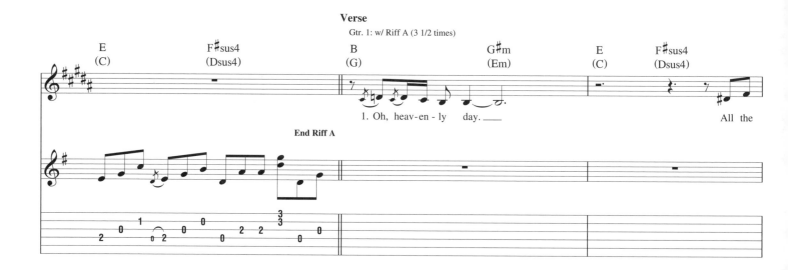

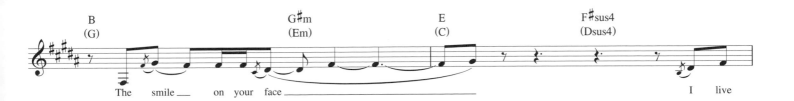

The smile ___ on your face _____ I live

on - ly to see. _____

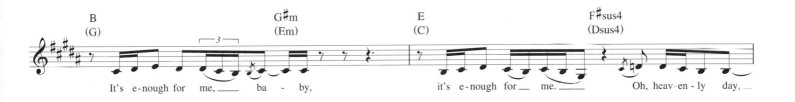

It's e-nough for me, ___ ba - by, it's e-nough for ___ me. ___ Oh, heav-en-ly day, ___

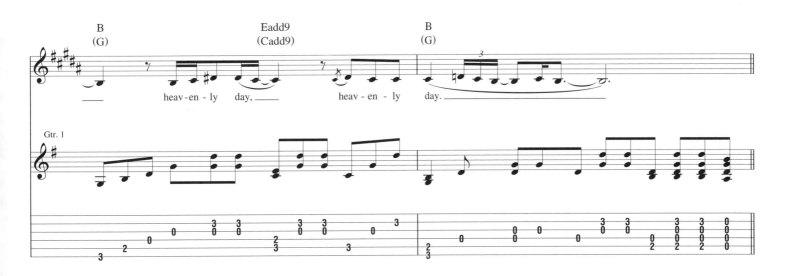

___ heav-en-ly day, ___ heav-en-ly day.

Gtr. 1

Chorus

To - mor-row may rain _____ with sor - row. _____

Rhy. Fig. 1

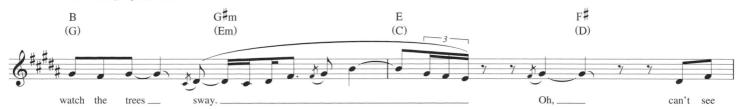

watch the trees ___ sway. _____ Oh, ___ can't see

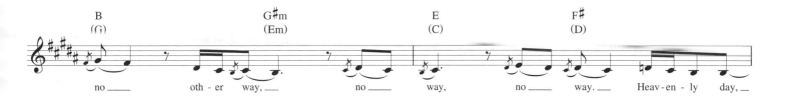

no ___ oth - er way, ___ no ___ way, no ___ way. ___ Heav - en - ly day, ___

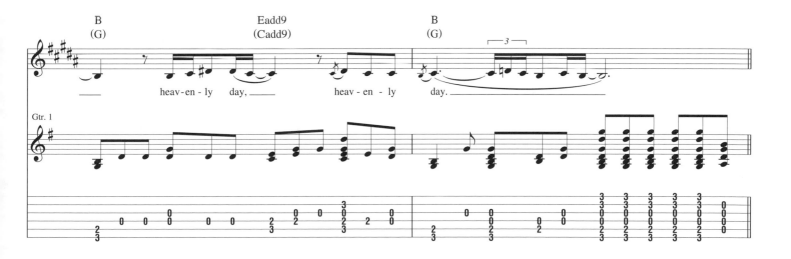

___ heav - en - ly day, ___ heav - en - ly day. _____

Chorus

Gtr. 1: w/ Rhy. Fig. 1

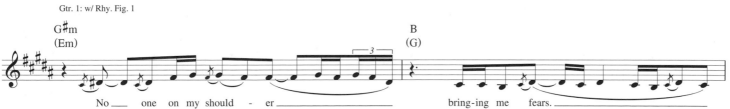

No ___ one on my should - er ___ bring - ing me fears. ___

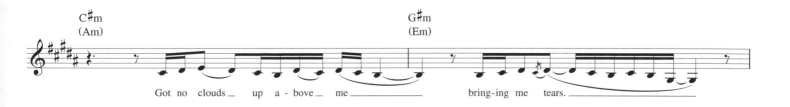

Got no clouds ___ up a - bove ___ me _____ bring - ing me tears. _____

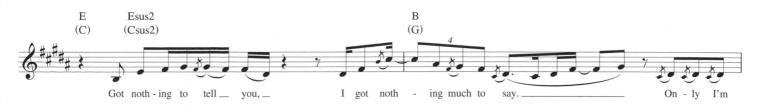

Got noth - ing to tell ___ you, I got noth - ing much to say. _____ On - ly I'm

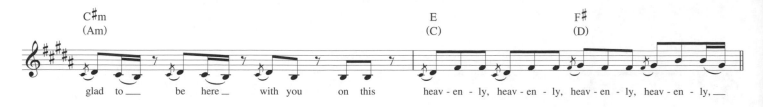

glad to __ be here __ with you on this heav-en-ly, heav-en-ly, heav-en-ly, heav-en-ly, __

Outro

Gtr. 1: w/ Rhy. Fig. 2 (3 times)

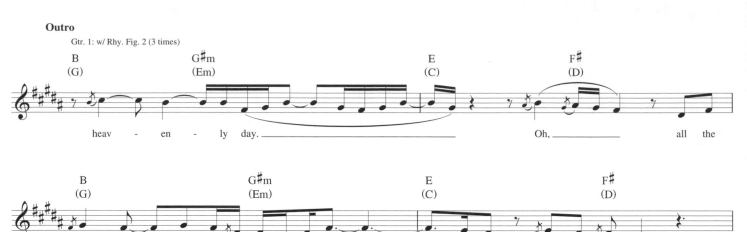

heav-en-ly day. __ Oh, __ all the

trou-ble __ gone a-way, __ oh, __

for a-while __ an-y-way, __ for a-while __ an-y-way. __ Heav-en-

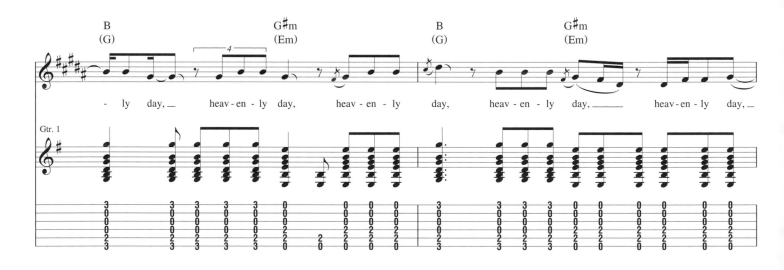

-ly day, __ heav-en-ly day, heav-en-ly day, heav-en-ly day, __ heav-en-ly day, __

Gtr. 1

Free time

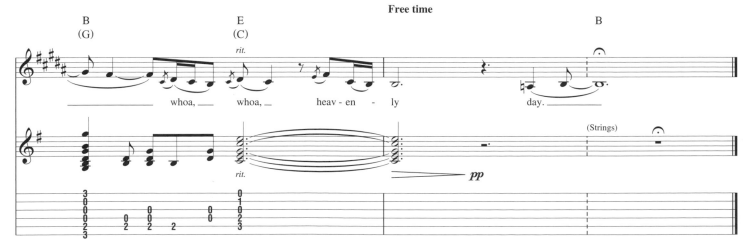

__ whoa, __ whoa, __ heav-en-ly day. __

(Strings)

rit.

pp

38

No Bad News

Words and Music by Patty Griffin

Open G tuning, Capo VI:
(low to high) D-G-D-G-B-D

*Symbols in parentheses represent chord names respective to capoed guitar.
 Symbols above reflect actual sounding chords. Capoed fret is "0" in tab.
 Chord symbols reflect basic harmony.

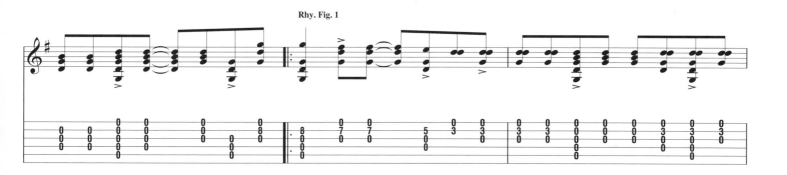

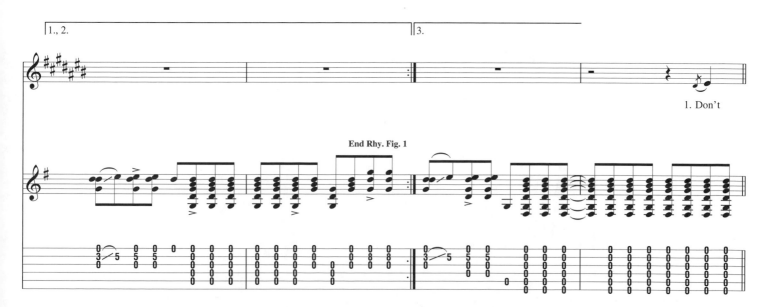

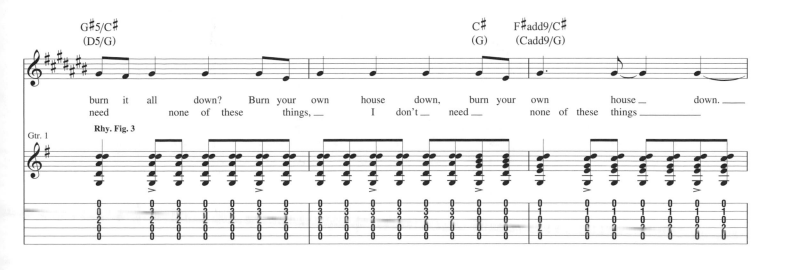

burn it all down? Burn your own house down, burn your own house ___ down. ___
need none of these things, ___ I don't ___ need ___ none of these things ___

Gtr. 1: w/ Rhy. Fig. 2 (last 4 meas.)

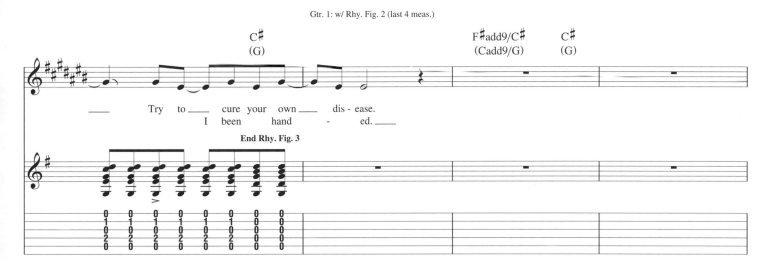

___ Try to ___ cure your own ___ dis-ease.
I been hand ___ ed. ___

Gtr. 1: w/ Rhy. Fig. 2 (1st 6 meas.)

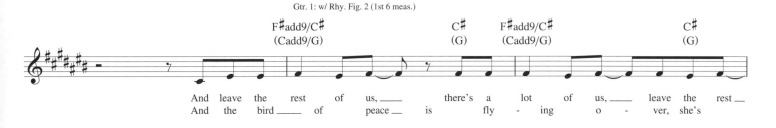

And leave the rest of us, ___ there's a lot of us, ___ leave the rest ___
And the bird ___ of peace ___ is fly - ing o - ver, she's

To Coda

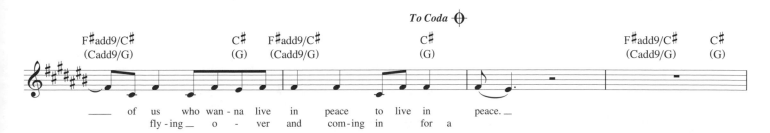

___ of us who wan - na live in peace to live in peace. ___
fly-ing ___ o - ver and com-ing in for a

Interlude

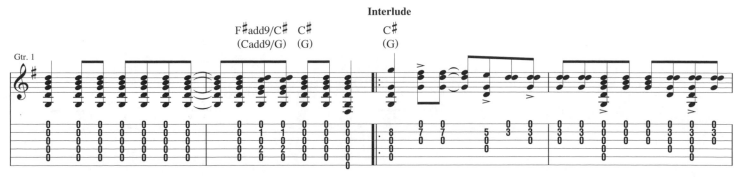

Verse

Gtr. 1: w/ Rhy. Fig. 2 (1st 2 meas., 3 times)

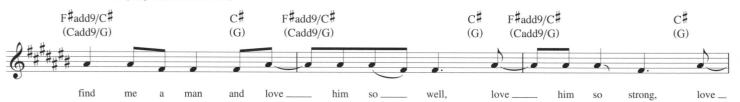

find me a man and love ___ him so ___ well, love ___ him so strong, love ___

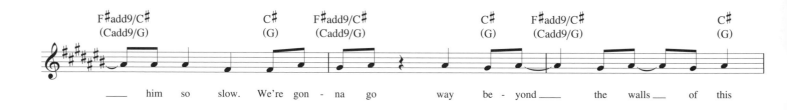

___ him so slow. We're gon - na go way be - yond ___ the walls ___ of this

Gtr. 1: w/ Rhy. Fig. 2 (last 4 meas.)

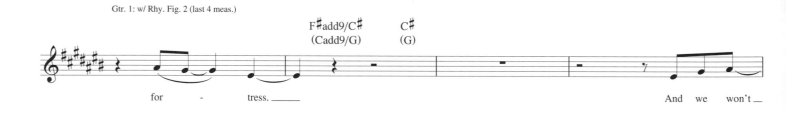

for - tress. ___ And we won't ___

Gtr. 1: w/ Rhy. Fig. 2 (1st 2 meas., 3 times)

___ be a - fraid ___ and won't ___ be a - fraid, ___ and though the dark - ness may

come our way ___ we won't ___ be a - fraid ___ to be a - live ___ an - y - more.

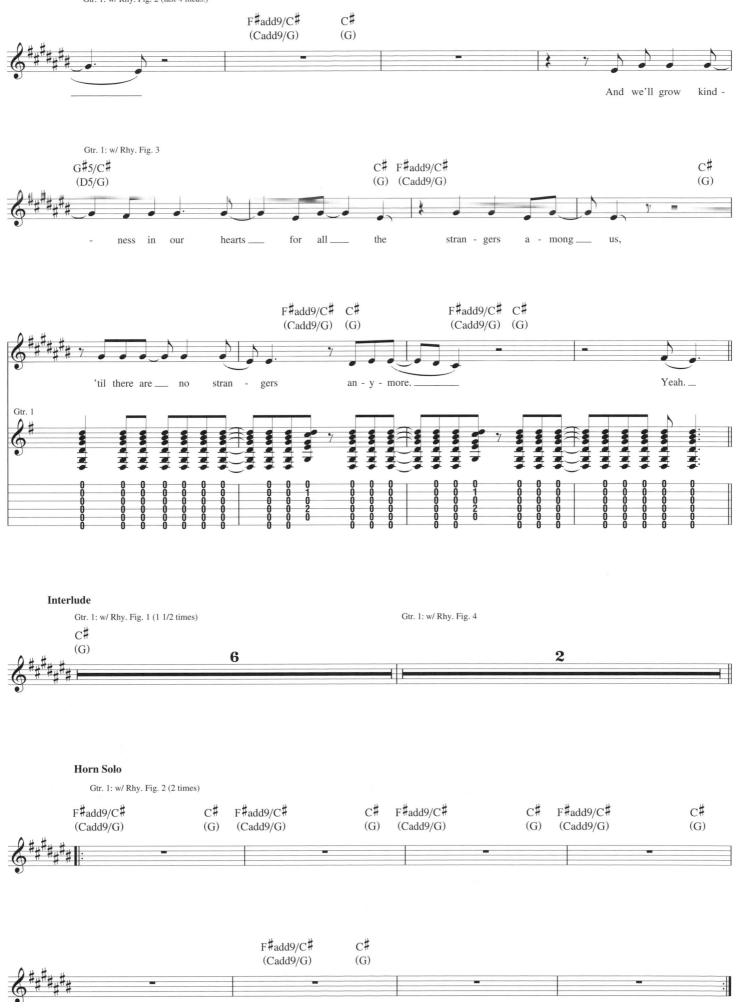

Interlude

Horn Solo

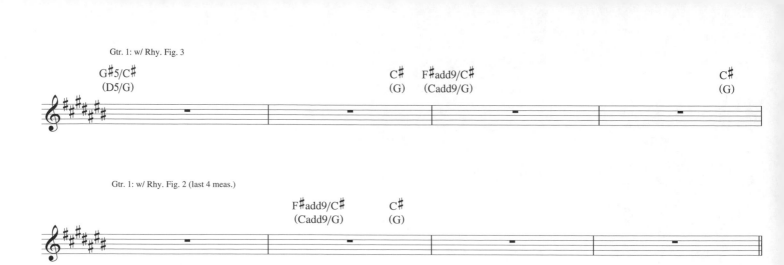

Gtr. 1: w/ Rhy. Fig. 3

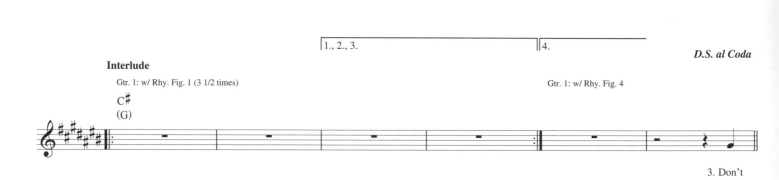

Gtr. 1: w/ Rhy. Fig. 2 (last 4 meas.)

Interlude

Gtr. 1: w/ Rhy. Fig. 1 (3 1/2 times)

Gtr. 1: w/ Rhy. Fig. 4

3. Don't

Coda

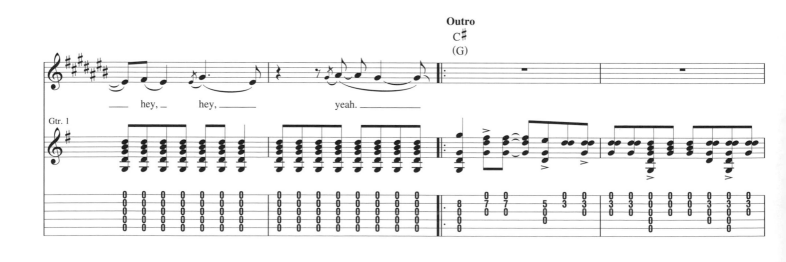

land - ing. _____ Hey,

Outro

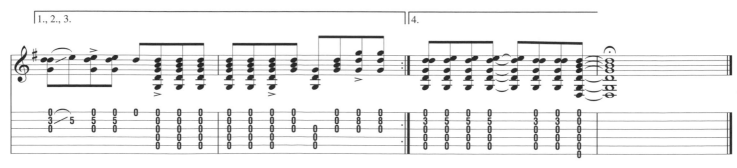

hey, hey, yeah.

Railroad Wings

Words and Music by Patty Griffin

Gtrs. 1 & 2: Capo VII

Gtr. 3: Open G tuning:
(low to high) D-G-D-G-B-D

*Symbols in parentheses represent chord names respective to capoed guitar.
Symbols above reflect actual sounding chords. Capoed fret is "0" in tab.
Chord symbols reflect implied harmony.

Verse

Gadd9
(Cadd9)

sil - ver __ train _____ all the way to Maine, __ on the

Gtrs. 1 & 2: w/ Riffs A & A1
Gtr. 3: w/ Riff B

things you don't know you __ know. ___ I thought an -

Cmaj7
(Fmaj7)

- ger told __ me __ what __ to do ___ with

Gadd9
(Cadd9)

emp - ti - ness ___ chas - ing __ me.

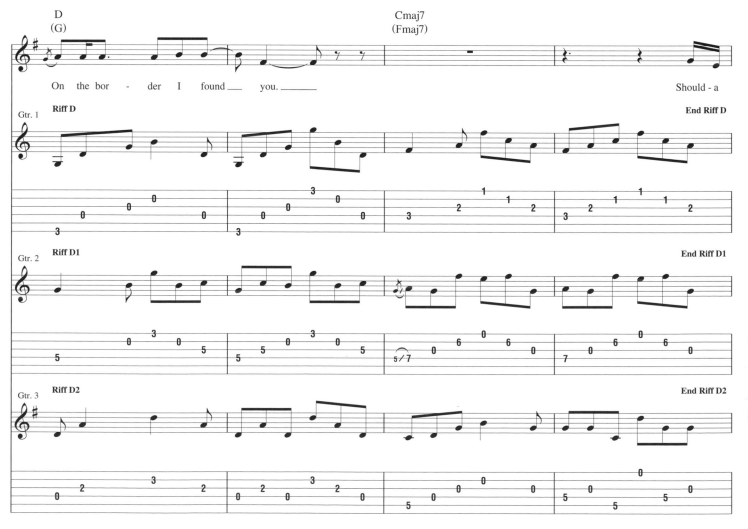

Gtr. 1: w/ Riff A (1st 4 meas., 2 times)
Gtr. 2: w/ Riff A1 (last 4 meas.)
Gtr. 3: w/ Riff C (2 times)

Gadd9
(Cadd9)

heard her ____ sing. _____

Gtr. 2: w/ Riff A1 (1st 4 meas.)

Rail - road wings. _____ This

Chorus

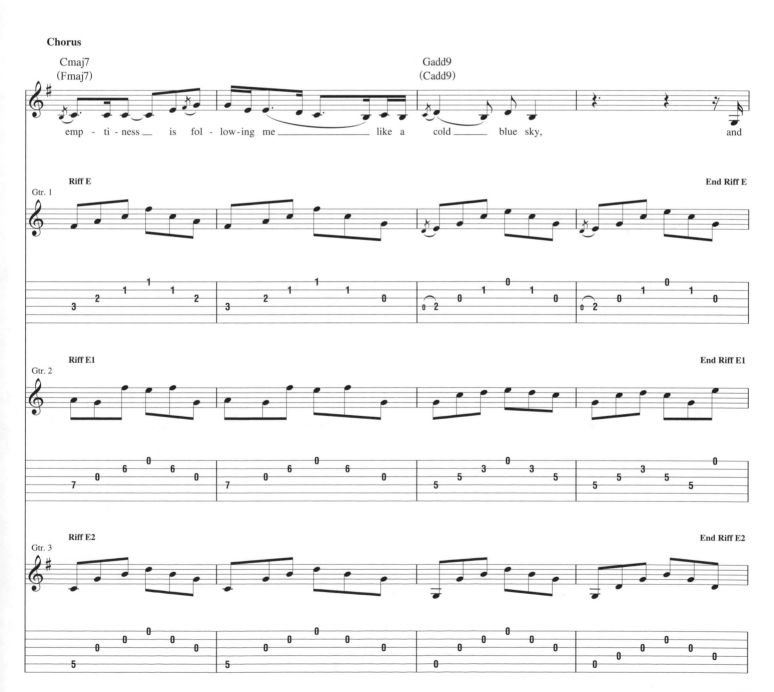

Cmaj7
(Fmaj7)

Gadd9
(Cadd9)

emp - ti - ness ____ is fol - low-ing me _____ like a cold ____ blue sky, and

Riff E   End Riff E
Gtr. 1

Riff E1   End Riff E1
Gtr. 2

Riff E2   End Riff E2
Gtr. 3

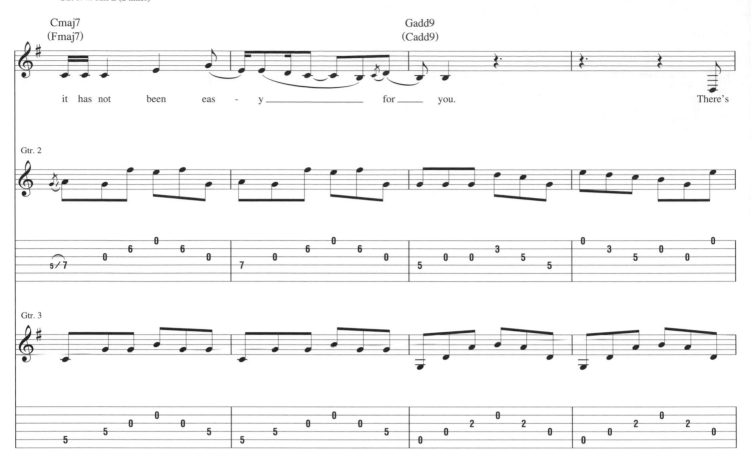

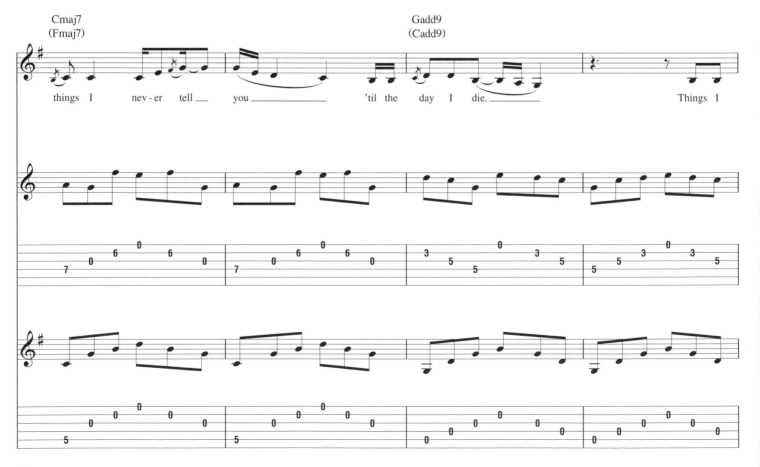

done,   I can nev - er un - do.

Gtr. 1: w/ Riff A (1st 4 meas., 2 times)

Hid - ing ev - 'ry - thing, _____

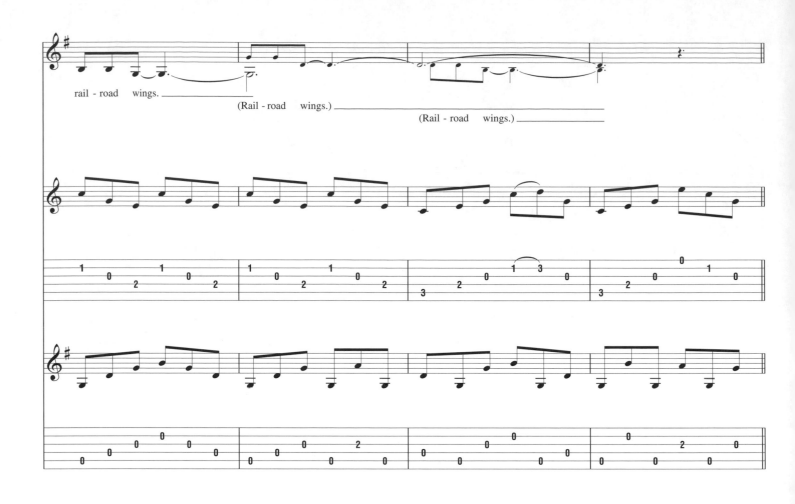

rail - road   wings. _____
(Rail - road   wings.) _____
(Rail - road   wings.) _____

Interlude

Gtrs. 1 & 3: w/ Riffs E & E2 (2 times)

Cmaj7
(Fmaj7)

Gadd9
(Cadd9)

Gtr. 2

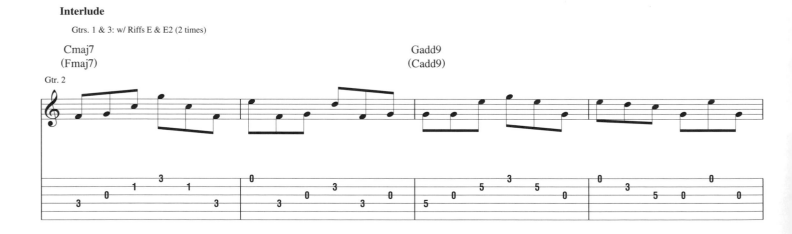

Cmaj7
(Fmaj7)

Gadd9
(Cadd9)

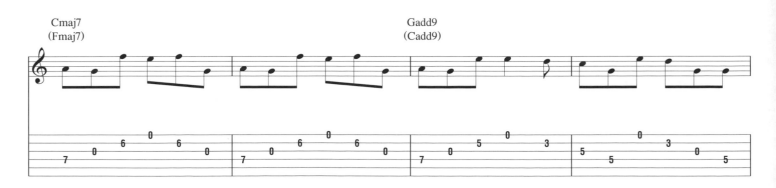

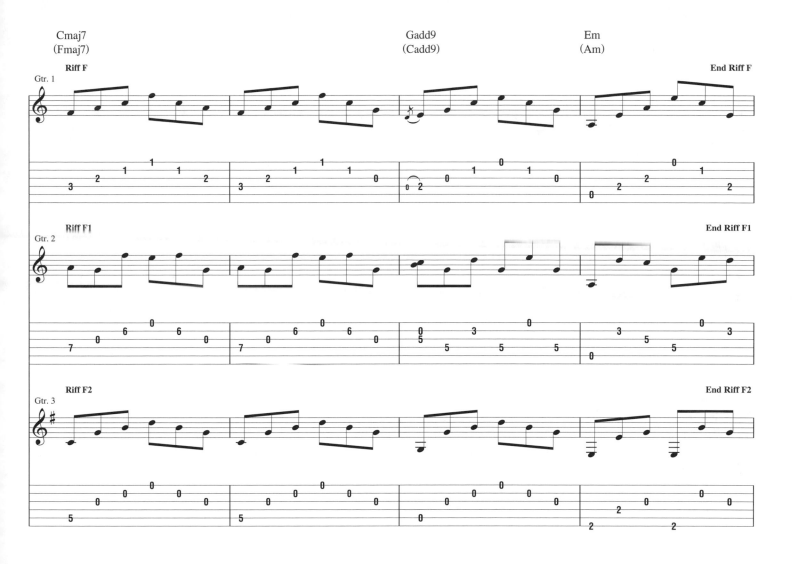

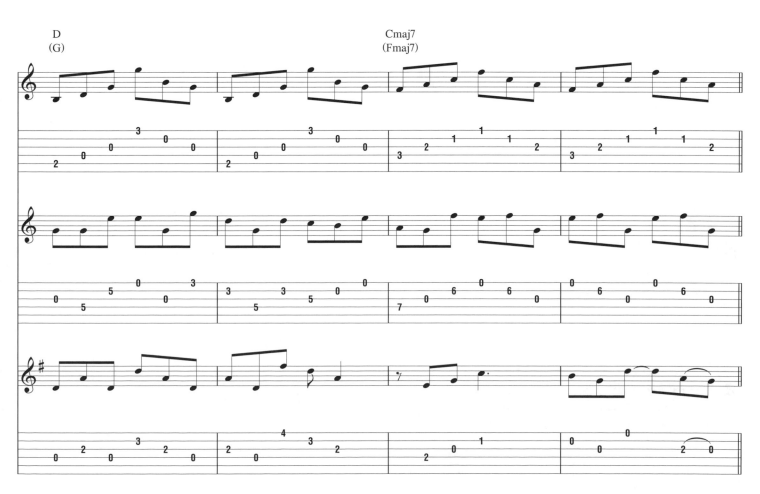

Verse

Gtrs. 1 & 2: w/ Riffs A & A1 (1st 4 meas.)
Gtr. 3: w/ Riff B (1st 4 meas.)

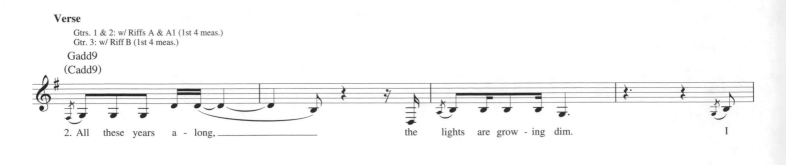

Gadd9
(Cadd9)

2. All these years a - long, _____ the lights are grow - ing dim. I

Gtrs. 1, 2 & 3: w/ Riffs E, E1 & E2

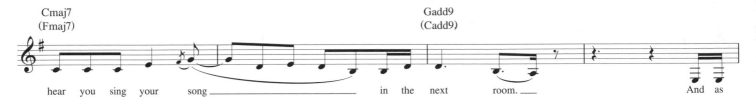

Cmaj7   Gadd9
(Fmaj7)   (Cadd9)

hear you sing your song _____ in the next room. _____ And as

Gtrs. 1, 2 & 3: w/ Riffs F, F1 & F2

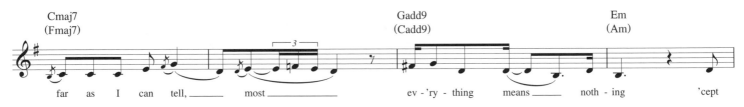

Cmaj7   Gadd9   Em
(Fmaj7)   (Cadd9)   (Am)

far as I can tell, _____ most _____ ev - 'ry - thing means _____ noth - ing 'cept

Gtrs. 1, 2 & 3: w/ Riffs D, D1 & D2

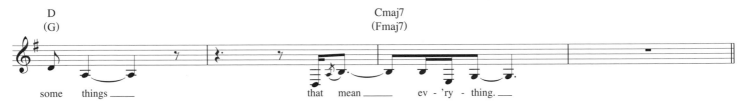

D   Cmaj7
(G)   (Fmaj7)

some things _____ that mean _____ ev - 'ry - thing. _____

Outro

Gtrs. 1 & 2: w/ Riffs A & A1 (1st 4 meas., 5 times)
Gtr. 3: w/ Riff B (1st 4 meas., 5 times)

Gadd9
(Cadd9)

Rail - road wings, _____

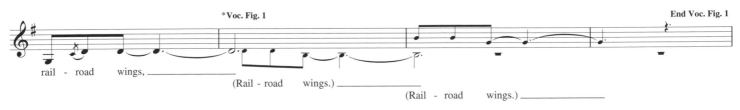

*Voc. Fig. 1   End Voc. Fig. 1

rail - road wings, _____
(Rail - road wings.) _____
(Rail - road wings.) _____

*Refers to downstemmed voc. only.

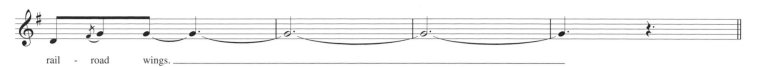

rail - road wings. _____

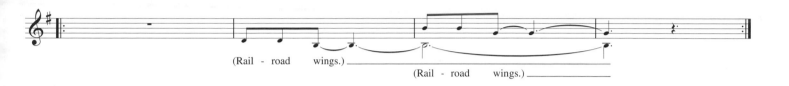

(Rail - road wings.) _____ (Rail - road wings.) _____

Rail - road wings. _____ (Rail - road wings.)

(Rail - road wings.) _____

Up to the Mountain (MLK Song)

Words and Music by Patty Griffin

Tune down 1/2 step:
(low to high) E♭-A♭-D♭-G♭-B♭-E♭

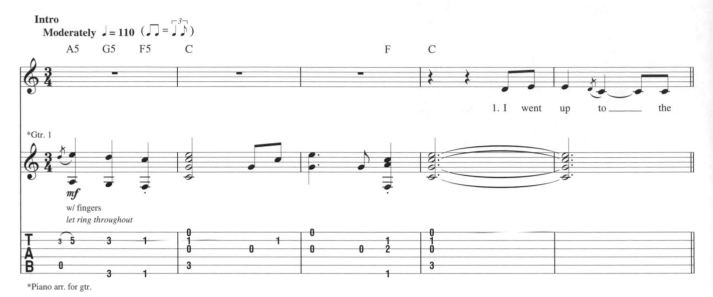

*Piano arr. for gtr.

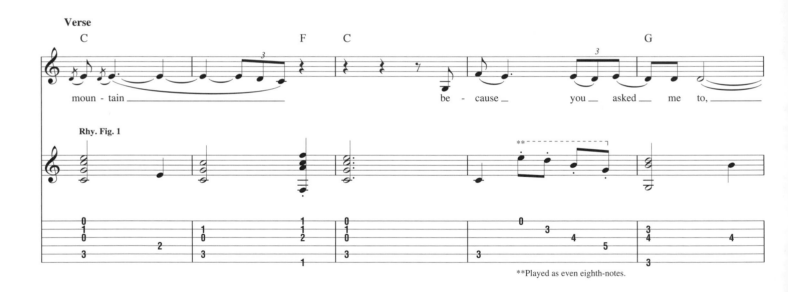

**Played as even eighth-notes.

Verse

Gtr. 1: w/ Rhy. Fig. 1

feel like ___ I ___ nev - er ___ been ___ noth - ing but tired, ___
(3.) - ley ___ just o - ver the moun -

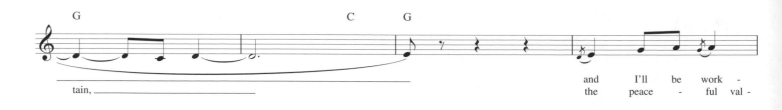

tain, ___ and I'll be work -
the peace - ful val -

Gtr. 1: w/ Rhy. Fig. 2

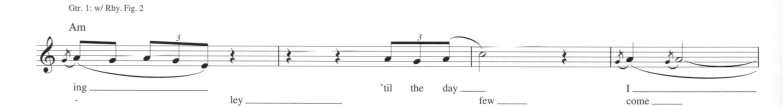

ing ___ 'til the day ___ I ___
- ley ___ few ___ come ___

___ ex - pire, ___ Some - times ___ I ___ lay ___
to know. I may nev - er get there ___

Gtr. 1: w/ Rhy. Fig. 1

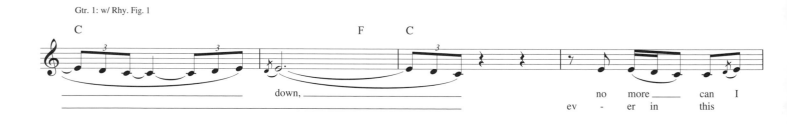

___ down, ___ no more ___ can I
ev - er in this

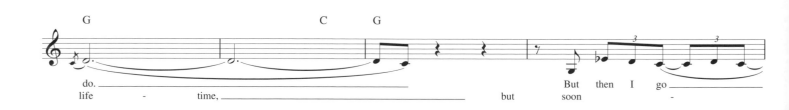

do. ___ But then I go ___
life - time, ___ but soon -

To Coda ⊕

Gtr. 1: w/ Rhy. Fig. 3

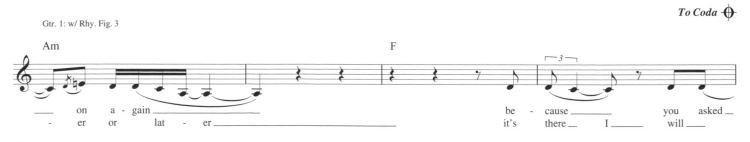

___ on a - gain ___ be - cause ___ you asked
- er or lat - er ___ it's there ___ I ___ will ___

Coda

Free time

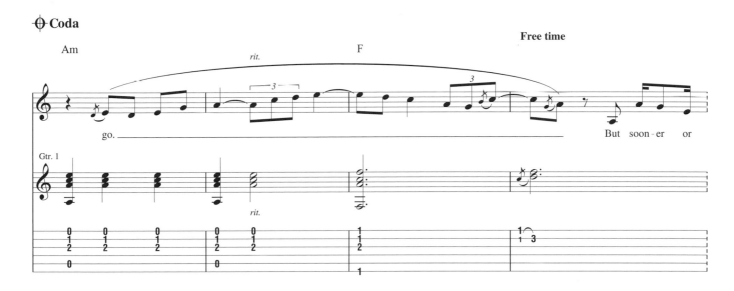

I Don't Ever Give Up

Words and Music by Patty Griffin

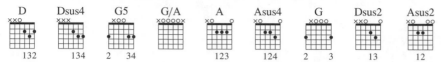

Gtr. 2: Open A tuning:
(low to high) E-A-E-A-C#-E

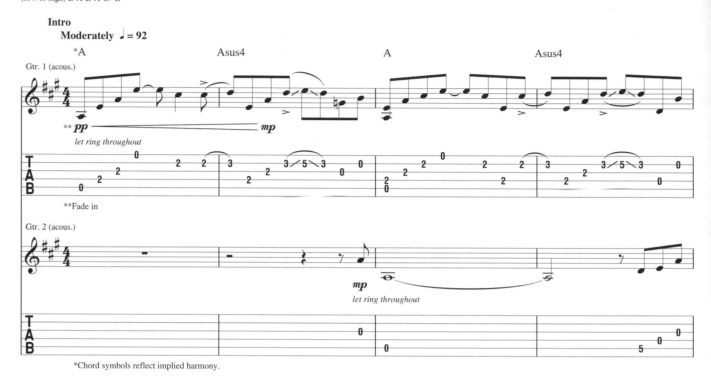

*Chord symbols reflect implied harmony.

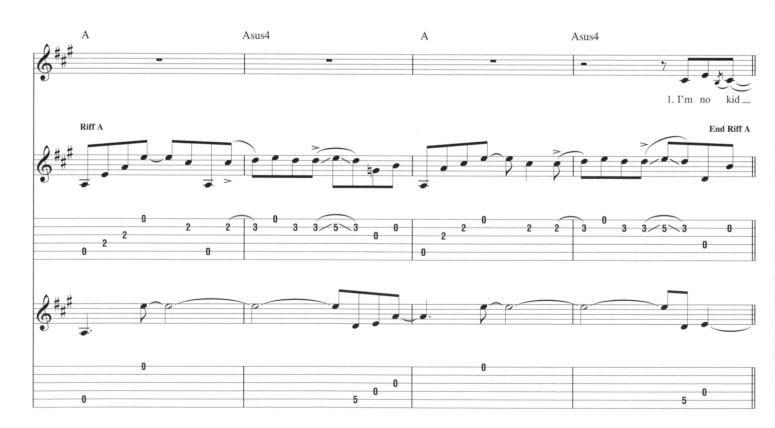

Verse

Gtr. 1: w/ Riff A (1 1/2 times)

in a kid's _____ game.

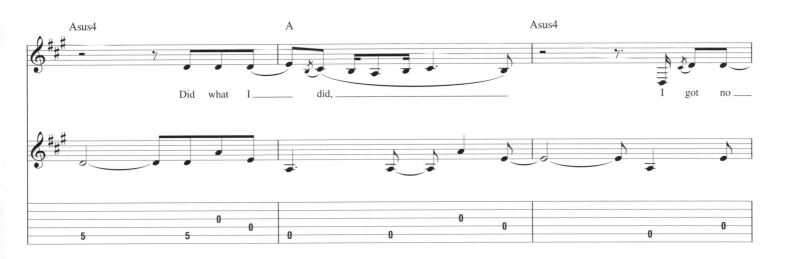

Did what I _____ did, _____ I got no _____

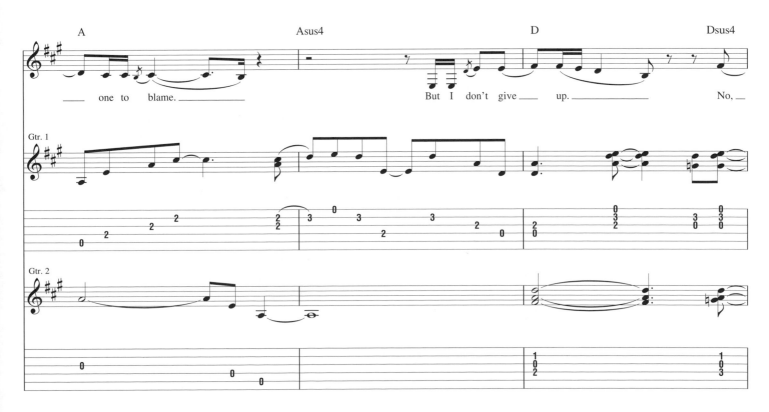

_____ one to blame. _____ But I don't give _____ up. _____ No, _____

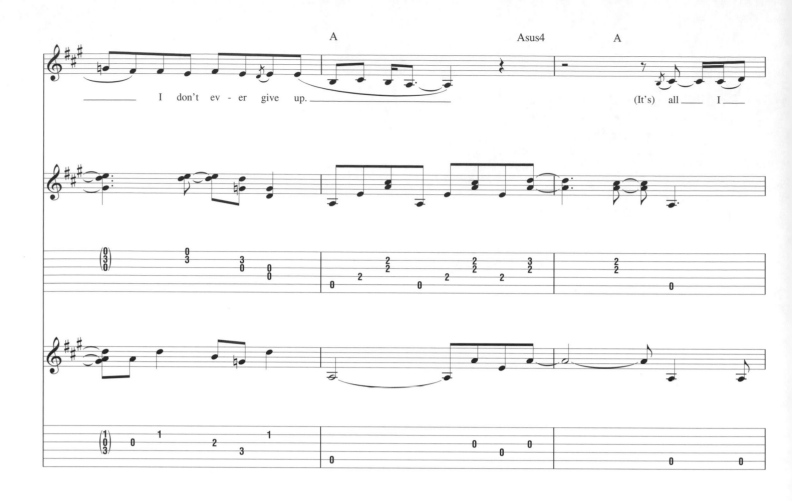

I don't ev - er give up. _____ (It's) all _____ I

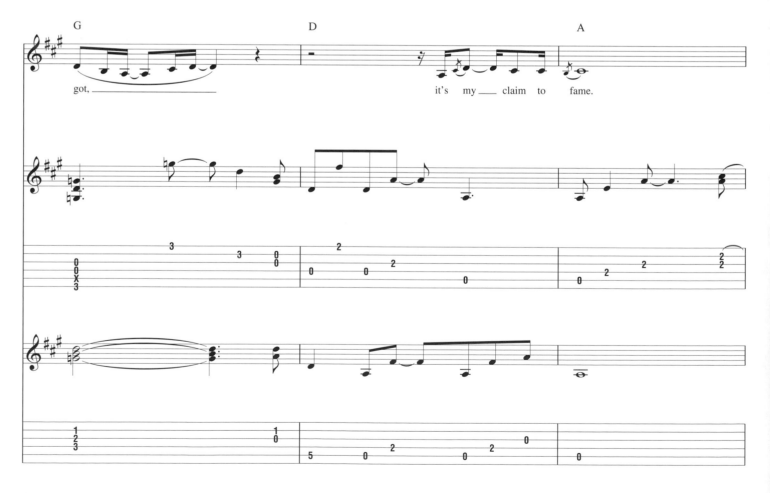

got, _____ it's my ___ claim to fame.

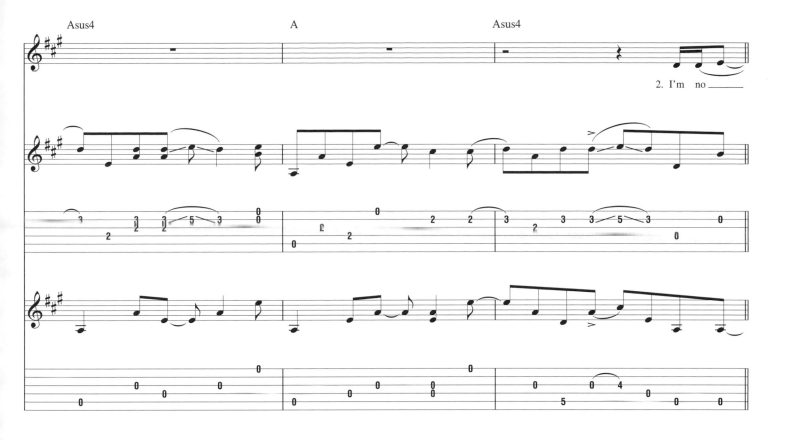

Verse

Gtr. 1: w/ Riff A (1 1/2 times)

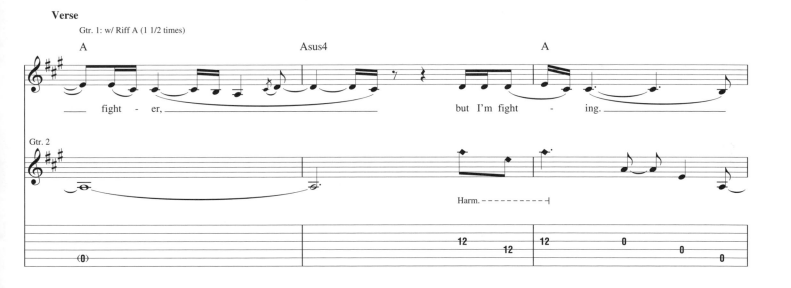

fight - er, but I'm fight - ing.

Gtr. 2

Harm.

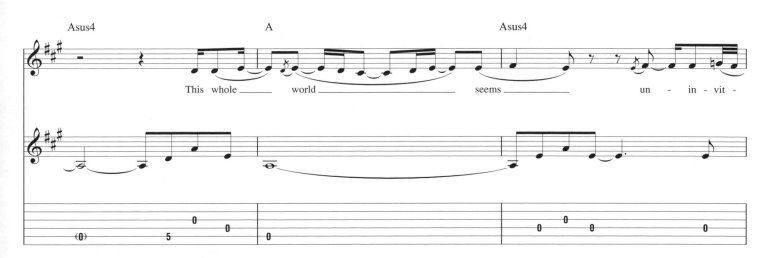

This whole world seems un - in - vit -

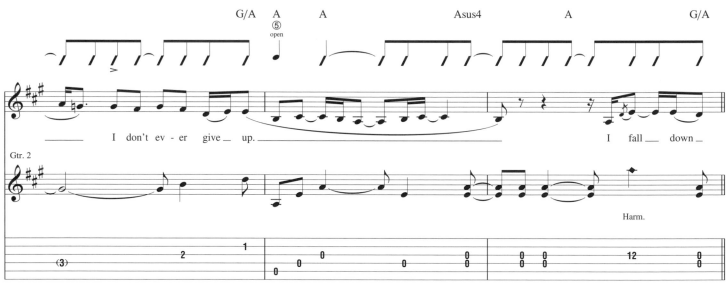

Interlude

Gtr. 1: w/ Riff A (2 times)

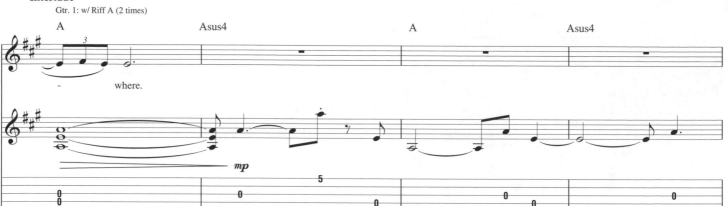

where.

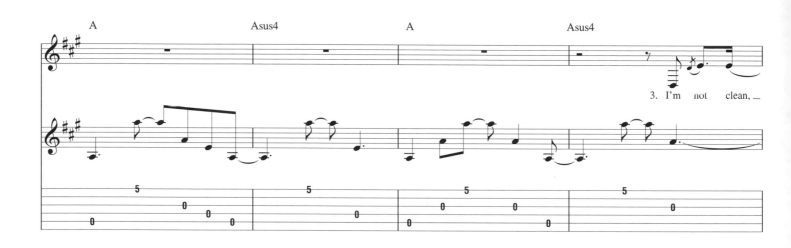

3. I'm not clean, ___

Verse

Gtr. 1: w/ Riff A (1 1/2 times)

I'm not washed ___ up. ___

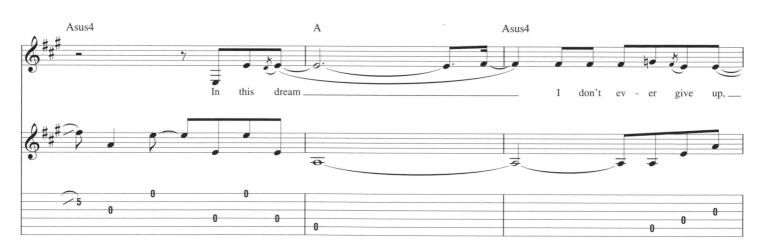

In this dream ___ I don't ev - er give up, ___

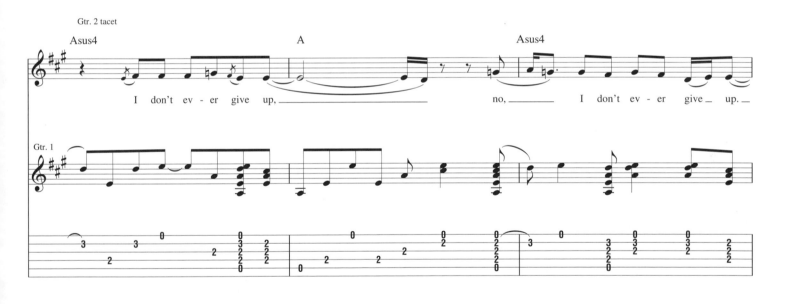

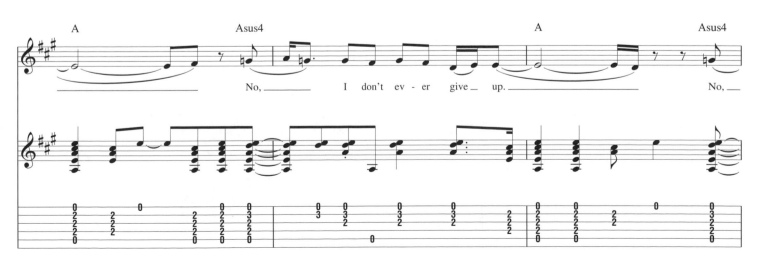

Outro

*Chord symbols reflect overall harmony.

Someone Else's Tomorrow

Words and Music by Patty Griffin

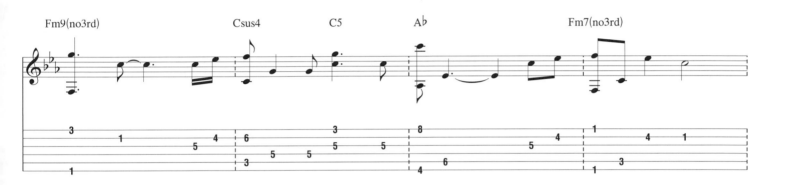

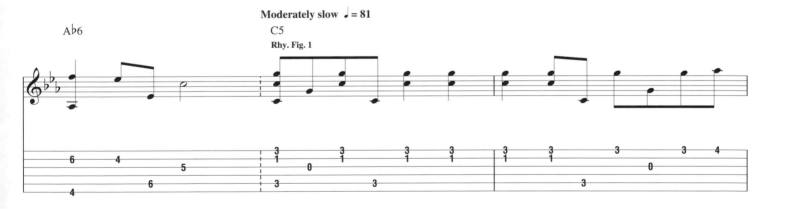

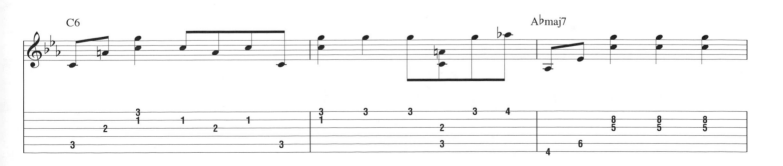

Fsus2

End Rhy. Fig. 1

Verse

C5

Rhy. Fig. 2

1. Have you ev - er been _____ bap - tized _____
2. The tall _____ and the ti - ny _____

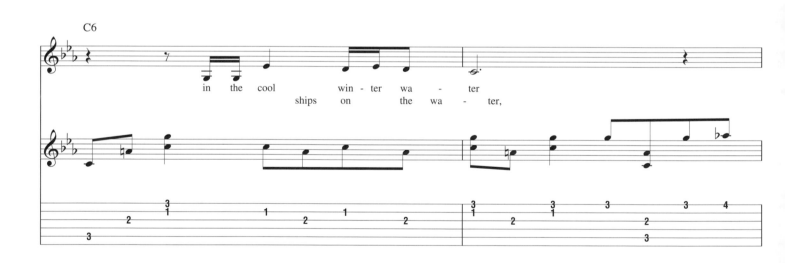

C6

in the cool win - ter wa - ter
ships on the wa - ter,

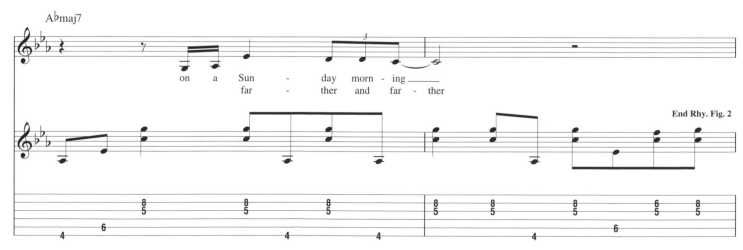

A♭maj7

on a Sun - day morn - ing _____
far - ther and far - ther

End Rhy. Fig. 2

Chorus

And all the mem - o - ries fade,

To Coda ⊕

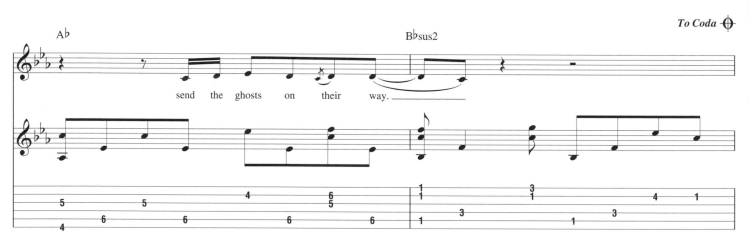

send the ghosts on their way.

Tell them they've had their day, _____ it's some - one else's _____ to - mor -

Interlude

Gtr. 1: w/ Rhy. Fig. 1 (1st 4 meas.)

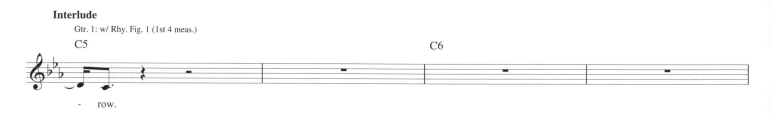

- row.

D.S. al Coda

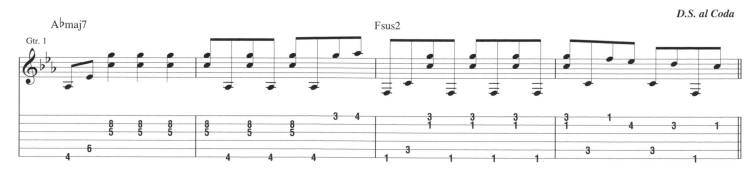

$\oplus$ Coda

Tell them they've had _____ their day, _____ some-one else's _____ to-mor-

Outro

Gtr. 1: w/ Rhy. Fig. 1

- row, some-one else's _____ to-mor - row.

Mm, _____ mm, _____

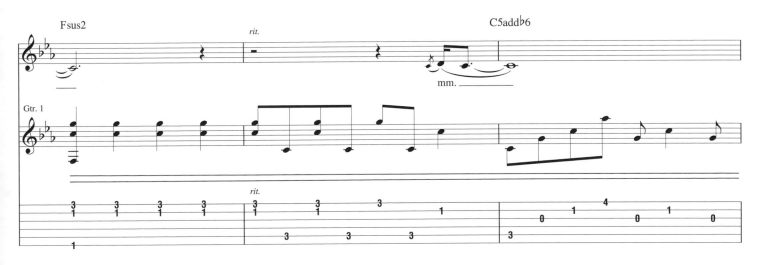

mm. _____

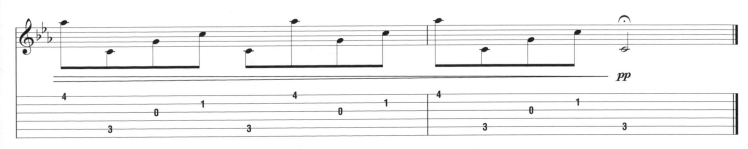

Crying Over

Words and Music by Patty Griffin

*Chords symbols reflect basic harmony.

1. Light __ it up, __

__ ba - by. __ Light up __ that fire, __

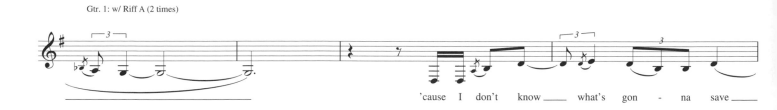

__ 'cause I don't know __ what's gon - na save __

Love leaves a mark

and life leaves

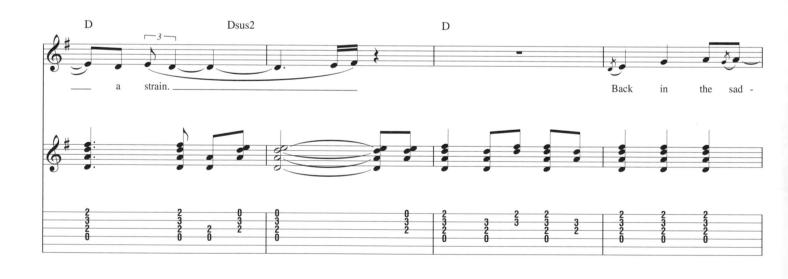

a strain. Back in the sad -

Gtr. 1: w/ Rhy. Fig. 4

-dle a - gain and a - gain.

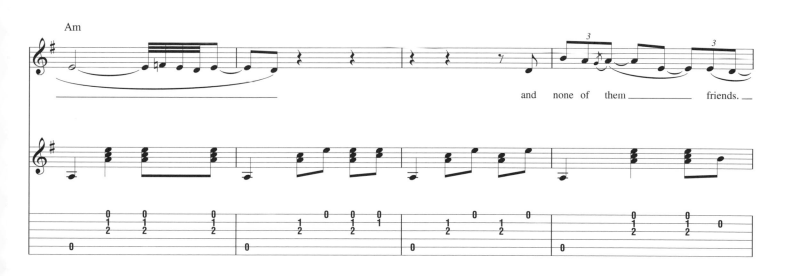

'cause I don't know___ what's gon - na___ save___

___ me _____   from the cold___

Gtr. 1

mf

D

___ now. _____   And these sor -

Chorus

Gtr. 1: w/ Rhy. Fig. 2

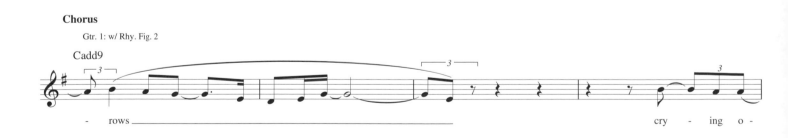

Cadd9

- rows _____   cry - ing o-

Gtr. 1: w/ Riff A

G

- ver, _____   and these sor -

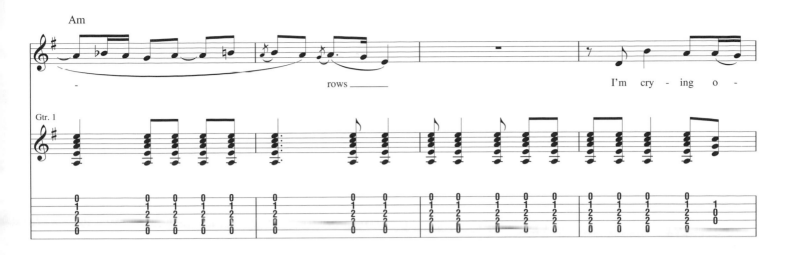

Outro

Guitar Notation Legend

Guitar music can be notated three different ways: on a *musical staff*, in *tablature*, and in *rhythm slashes*.

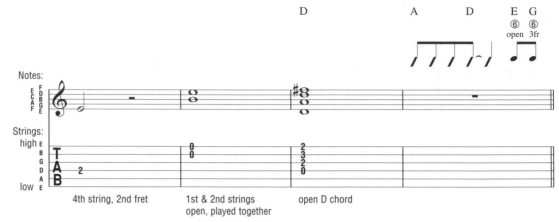

RHYTHM SLASHES are written above the staff. Strum chords in the rhythm indicated. Use the chord diagrams found at the top of the first page of the transcription for the appropriate chord voicings. Round noteheads indicate single notes.

THE MUSICAL STAFF shows pitches and rhythms and is divided by bar lines into measures. Pitches are named after the first seven letters of the alphabet.

TABLATURE graphically represents the guitar fingerboard. Each horizontal line represents a string, and each number represents a fret.

4th string, 2nd fret

1st & 2nd strings open, played together

open D chord

Definitions for Special Guitar Notation

HALF-STEP BEND: Strike the note and bend up 1/2 step.

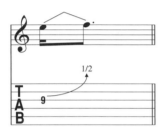

WHOLE-STEP BEND: Strike the note and bend up one step.

GRACE NOTE BEND: Strike the note and immediately bend up as indicated.

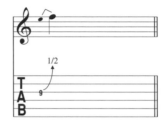

SLIGHT (MICROTONE) BEND: Strike the note and bend up 1/4 step.

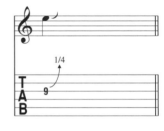

BEND AND RELEASE: Strike the note and bend up as indicated, then release back to the original note. Only the first note is struck.

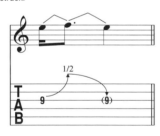

PRE-BEND: Bend the note as indicated, then strike it.

PRE-BEND AND RELEASE: Bend the note as indicated. Strike it and release the bend back to the original note.

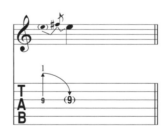

UNISON BEND: Strike the two notes simultaneously and bend the lower note up to the pitch of the higher.

VIBRATO: The string is vibrated by rapidly bending and releasing the note with the fretting hand.

WIDE VIBRATO: The pitch is varied to a greater degree by vibrating with the fretting hand.

HAMMER-ON: Strike the first (lower) note with one finger, then sound the higher note (on the same string) with another finger by fretting it without picking.

PULL-OFF: Place both fingers on the notes to be sounded. Strike the first note and without picking, pull the finger off to sound the second (lower) note.

LEGATO SLIDE: Strike the first note and then slide the same fret-hand finger up or down to the second note. The second note is not struck.

SHIFT SLIDE: Same as legato slide, except the second note is struck.

TRILL: Very rapidly alternate between the notes indicated by continuously hammering on and pulling off.

TAPPING: Hammer ("tap") the fret indicated with the pick-hand index or middle finger and pull off to the note fretted by the fret hand.

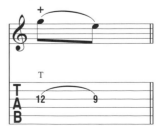

NATURAL HARMONIC: Strike the note while the fret-hand lightly touches the string directly over the fret indicated.

PINCH HARMONIC: The note is fretted normally and a harmonic is produced by adding the edge of the thumb or the tip of the index finger of the pick hand to the normal pick attack.

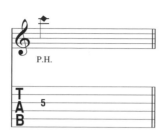

HARP HARMONIC: The note is fretted normally and a harmonic is produced by gently resting the pick hand's index finger directly above the indicated fret (in parentheses) while the pick hand's thumb or pick assists by plucking the appropriate string.

PICK SCRAPE: The edge of the pick is rubbed down (or up) the string, producing a scratchy sound.

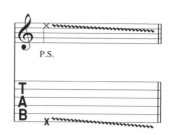

MUFFLED STRINGS: A percussive sound is produced by laying the fret hand across the string(s) without depressing, and striking them with the pick hand.

PALM MUTING: The note is partially muted by the pick hand lightly touching the string(s) just before the bridge.

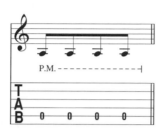

RAKE: Drag the pick across the strings indicated with a single motion.

TREMOLO PICKING: The note is picked as rapidly and continuously as possible.

ARPEGGIATE: Play the notes of the chord indicated by quickly rolling them from bottom to top.

VIBRATO BAR DIVE AND RETURN: The pitch of the note or chord is dropped a specified number of steps (in rhythm), then returned to the original pitch.

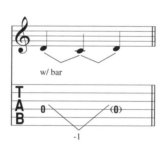

VIBRATO BAR SCOOP: Depress the bar just before striking the note, then quickly release the bar.

VIBRATO BAR DIP: Strike the note and then immediately drop a specified number of steps, then release back to the original pitch.

Additional Musical Definitions

(accent) • Accentuate note (play it louder).

(accent) • Accentuate note with great intensity.

(staccato) • Play the note short.

• Downstroke

• Upstroke

D.S. al Coda • Go back to the sign (𝄋), then play until the measure marked "*To Coda,*" then skip to the section labelled "**Coda.**"

D.C. al Fine • Go back to the beginning of the song and play until the measure marked "*Fine*" (end).

Rhy. Fig. • Label used to recall a recurring accompaniment pattern (usually chordal).

Riff • Label used to recall composed, melodic lines (usually single notes) which recur.

Fill • Label used to identify a brief melodic figure which is to be inserted into the arrangement.

Rhy. Fill • A chordal version of a Fill.

tacet • Instrument is silent (drops out).

• Repeat measures between signs.

• When a repeated section has different endings, play the first ending only the first time and the second ending only the second time.

NOTE: Tablature numbers in parentheses mean:
1. The note is being sustained over a system (note in standard notation is tied), or
2. The note is sustained, but a new articulation (such as a hammer-on, pull-off, slide or vibrato) begins, or
3. The note is a barely audible "ghost" note (note in standard notation is also in parentheses).

GUITAR RECORDED VERSIONS®

Guitar Recorded Versions® are note-for-note transcriptions of guitar music taken directly off recordings. This series, one of the most popular in print today, features some of the greatest guitar players and groups from blues and rock to country and jazz.

Guitar Recorded Versions are transcribed by the best transcribers in the business. Every book contains notes and tablature. Visit www.halleonard.com for our complete selection.

AUTHENTIC TRANSCRIPTIONS
WITH NOTES AND TABLATURE

HAL•LEONARD GUITAR PLAY-ALONG®

This series will help you play your favorite songs quickly and easily. **INCLUDES TAB** Just follow the tab and listen to the CD to hear how the guitar should sound, and then play along using the separate backing tracks. Mac or PC users can also slow down the tempo without changing pitch by using the CD in their computer. The melody and lyrics are included in the book so that you can sing or simply follow along.